IMAGES
of America

TACOMA'S PARKS

Melissa McGinnis, Doreen Beard-Simpkins,
and the Metropolitan Park District of Tacoma

ARCADIA
PUBLISHING

Published by Arcadia Publishing
Charleston SC, Chicago IL, Portsmouth NH, San Francisco CA

Printed in the United States of America

Library of Congress Catalog Card Number: 2007922159

For all general information contact Arcadia Publishing at:
Telephone 843-853-2070
Fax 843-853-0044
E-mail sales@arcadiapublishing.com
For customer service and orders:
Toll-Free 1-888-313-2665

Visit us on the Internet at www.arcadiapublishing.com

Ebenezer Rhys Roberts (1854–1918), a noted Welsh gardener, was an immigrant to the young city of Tacoma. As the superintendent of parks, he was responsible for much of the early beautification of the city. Roberts's deft hand planted all of Tacoma's first parks, and in his retirement, he served as a beloved master gardener to whom the city turned for horticultural wisdom. (Courtesy Jean Insel Robeson.)

CONTENTS

ACKNOWLEDGMENTS

The citizens of Tacoma have made this book possible. They have supported their parks since 1907 by electing the Board of Park Commissioners, by property tax assessments, and by availing themselves of the sheer pleasure of the rich variety of park retreats and experiences that have evolved in this city over the past 100 years. Many citizens also provided wonderful reminiscences and family photographs, and to them we are singularly indebted for their valuable contribution to the historical record.

We gratefully acknowledge the present Board of Park Commissioners—Larry Dahl, Ryan Mello, Aaron Pointer, Tim Reid, and Victoria Woodards—as well as Metro Parks Tacoma executive director Jack C. Wilson and director of recreation Shon Sylvia, who have encouraged this project. Indeed we pay tribute to all of our Metro Parks Tacoma colleagues, both present and past, for their dedication and service across all departments of the agency. They truly serve the Metro Parks Tacoma mission to create healthy opportunities to play, learn, and grow. In particular, communications coordinator Sheree Trefry deserves special recognition for her cheerful assistance with technical preparation of the archival photographs.

The exemplary research collections of the Tacoma Public Library Northwest Room (TPL), the Washington State Historical Society (WSHS), and the Tacoma Historical Society (THS) merit particular mention. Tacoma is remarkably the richer for them all and for the proficient assistance rendered by their very capable staffs. Thank you Brian Kamens, Robert Schuler, Jody Grimm, Elaine Miller, Joy Werlink, and Dale Wirsing, respectively.

Lastly we salute the many unsung secretaries to the Board of Park Commissioners for keeping decades' worth of official minutes, with particular gratitude reserved for those who indexed. And, as ever, the profound thanks of all historians are bestowed upon those who write down the names, dates, locations, and occasions on the back of every photograph. Always in pencil, please.

INTRODUCTION

Public parks and recreational opportunities have been important to the citizens of Tacoma since the city's incorporation in 1884. The story of Tacoma's parks begins, as does so much of the city's early history, with the arrival of the Northern Pacific Railway Company. The community's actual origin dates to the late 1860s with the establishment of Tacoma City, a small hamlet of settlers near today's Old Town neighborhood. These settlers hoped that their locale would become the Puget Sound terminus of the Northern Pacific rails. The railway did indeed choose Tacoma over Seattle in 1873, but not the Tacoma City site. Instead they chose a different town site called New Tacoma in the area that developed into today's downtown. The two fledgling communities, separated by only a few miles along the Commencement Bay shoreline, united in 1884 as the city of Tacoma, numbering some 4,000 citizens and one park.

Parks were part of the Tacoma landscape from the beginning. Just months before the two Tacomas joined to form one city, wealthy civic booster Clinton P. Ferry donated to the community a small parcel of land in an area he was platting for residential development. This property was to be developed as a park, setting an example of the importance of such spaces to a city's beauty, livability, and enjoyment. It became known as Ferry Park, Tacoma's first. Ferry, along with other prominent individuals and business interests, understood that the development of parks was vital to Tacoma's well being and image, particularly when advertising their young city's charms to prospects back east. Soon after Ferry made his donation, other civic benefactors followed suit, giving birth to Tacoma's cherished system of public green spaces.

Planning for Tacoma's parks in this early era also figures in an intriguing historical "what-if." In 1873, Charles B. Wright, president of the Tacoma Land Company, invited Frederick Law Olmsted (1822–1903) to submit plans for laying out the city of Tacoma. Olmsted, hailed today as the founder of American landscape architecture, was at the time one of the designers of New York City's Central Park. His concepts for creating harmonious public landscapes were making him increasingly prominent in later-19th-century America. Olmsted submitted a radical city plan, never adopted by Tacoma, with very few square city blocks and several large parcels of park acreage that followed the city's natural land contours rather than a strict alignment to a grid system. Even though Tacoma did not choose to follow Olmsted's plan, his philosophy and ideas of park creation certainly influenced the aesthetic of early Tacoma landscape designers, who were later instrumental in the layout and planting of Wright Park and Point Defiance Park.

From 1884 to 1890, a committee of Tacoma city council members managed the fledgling collection of parks. By 1890, Tacoma's mayor, Stuart Rice, decided that the city needed a separate board to manage the growing park system, by then numbering more than 700 acres. On June 7, 1890, Rice appointed the first Board of Park Commissioners, confirmed by the city council, to serve one-year terms or "until their successors are appointed and qualified."

This first Board of Park Commissioners immediately hired landscape architect Edward Otto Schwagerl, a native of Bavaria, to design plans for the development of Wright Park as well as Point Defiance Park. They also hired Ebenezer Rhys Roberts, a well-known horticulturalist from Wales working at Wapato Lake Park—a privately owned estate in Tacoma at the time—to oversee the implementation of Schwagerl's designs for Wright and Point Defiance Parks, as well as to manage the improvements at McKinley, Puget, and Lincoln Parks.

In 1907, former mayor Stuart Rice, now serving as president of the Board of Park Commissioners, realized the urgent need for a separate base of tax support exclusively for parks. This became especially apparent following the 1905 acquisition of the Point Defiance Park property. For years, the appointed board had struggled to get the necessary funding from the city council to operate the growing park system. A tireless advocate, Rice lobbied the state legislature to pass a resolution allowing cities to set up independent park districts. Once the legislature passed the bill and the governor signed it into law, the citizens of Tacoma voted to establish a municipal park district with independent taxing authority governed by an elected board of five park commissioners. This vote, on April 2, 1907, created the Metropolitan Park District of Tacoma as a municipal entity separate from the City of Tacoma. Now known as Metro Parks Tacoma, the agency celebrates its centennial in 2007 as the steward of Tacoma's treasury of parks and recreation amenities. Incidentally, not all parks in Tacoma are under the jurisdiction of the park district. A number are the property of the City of Tacoma, even though they may be operated and maintained by the park district.

In the early decades of the 20th century, Tacoma's parks witnessed the expansion of evolving national concepts of how outdoor public spaces should be used. Parks were still to be green retreats, but public sentiment now embraced the notion that parks should also increase the public good by providing locations and programs for the growing interest in structured leisure time. By the 1920s, the Metropolitan Park District of Tacoma had established cooperative agreements with the Tacoma School District and other agencies to offer an extraordinary variety of organized recreational programs in parks across the city. Children spent their summer days learning a variety of arts and crafts, performing in plays and other theatrical events, playing baseball, volleyball, tennis or croquet, or competing in bubble-gum-blowing contests and pet parades. Over the decades, these simple programs for the wholesome recreation of young people evolved into today's sophisticated facilities and opportunities for organized league sports, aquatics, recreation, fitness, arts, and travel for citizens of all ages.

Finally, a lasting component embraced by Tacoma's parks is the evolving professional emphasis on education. The horticultural intricacies of trial gardens and greenhouses, the environmental interpretation of the Tacoma Nature Center, the zoological collections as conserved by Northwest Trek and the Point Defiance Zoo and Aquarium, and the historical heritage of Fort Nisqually Living History Museum and other historic assets—all these aspects testify that education is now established and intertwined with conservation and recreation as one of the core values of Metro Parks Tacoma at the start of the 21st century.

Tacoma's parks make this a community of remarkable distinction in which to live, and its citizens are justifiably proud and protective of their heritage. With that in mind, the authors regret that this volume does not contain enough pages to illustrate each and every park and program. Instead this record of selected historical images paints a broad canvas of the history, variety, and depth of civic park amenities that Tacomans have enjoyed for over 100 years.

One

Tacoma's First Parks

When the first elected Board of Park Commissioners took office in 1907, Tacoma already boasted nine public parks. One of the nine, Spanaway Lake Park, was technically outside the city limits; however, the Metropolitan Park District of Tacoma managed the park until 1959, at which time it deeded the property to Pierce County. These original parks were spread throughout all geographic regions of the city and ranged in size from Ferry Park's three-quarters of an acre to Point Defiance Park's 640 acres.

Both Ferry Park (1883) and Puget Park (1888) were gifts to Tacoma from the men developing new additions to the growing community. The Northern Pacific Railway and its real estate subsidiary, the Tacoma Land Company, also had the commendable foresight to set aside land for park purposes; these parks include Wright Park (1886), Lincoln Park (1889), Fireman's Park (1891), and McKinley Park (1901).

Point Defiance Park was known as Point Defiance Military Reserve until 1888, when the U.S. federal government voted to allow the city of Tacoma to develop the property as a public park. It was not until 1905, however, that Pres. Theodore Roosevelt signed the legislation that formally turned over the acreage of Point Defiance Park to Tacoma. In that same year, the city government conveyed management of South Park to the Board of Park Commissioners.

Wapato Lake Park actually constituted a 10th park in Tacoma in 1907, but the Metropolitan Park District did not own or manage it until 1920. R. F. Radebaugh, owner of the *Tacoma Weekly Ledger* newspaper, privately established this park in 1889 as a part of his real estate and streetcar enterprises in the southern reaches of town. As he platted the land around Wapato Lake for development of private homes, Radebaugh also set aside areas for the public, encouraging people to ride the Fern Hill Streetcar out to Wapato Lake to swim, boat, dance, and relax.

These first parks are the cornerstones of Tacoma's extensive park system. Spread throughout the city, they stand as testimony to Tacoma's belief in the importance of public green spaces.

Located on South Fourteenth Street between Sheridan and Cushman Avenues, Ferry Park bears the distinction of being the first parcel of land specifically set aside for park purposes in Tacoma. Pictured here enjoying the outdoors, Clinton P. Ferry, the self-styled "Duke of Tacoma," was born in Indiana but headed west, settling in Tacoma in 1873 and making his fortune in adroit real estate investments. (Courtesy WSHS.)

Ferry donated the land in 1883 and platted the neighborhood to accommodate his namesake park's oval shape. In 1902, he ordered statuary from Europe to beautify the tract, including sphinxes, griffins, and a lioness with her cubs. Two statues were removed from the park some time in the spring of 1928, apparently due to neighbors who objected to the depiction of nursing cubs; the statues' fate remains unknown. (Courtesy Thomas Stenger.)

Ferry Park was among the first parks in Tacoma to have a supervised public playground program during the summer months, beginning in the 1920s, as the Metropolitan Park District invested in the growing national recreation movement. In 1928, the Kiwanis Club donated $2,000 for the construction of a field house in which to hold art classes and other activities and to fence the perimeter of the park.

Ferry Park was a scene of controversy in the summer of 1948, as neighborhood children protested the loss of play equipment. It had been removed earlier in the decade due to pressure from residents bordering the park, who apparently preferred only green grass. Ferry Park continued to languish for a time before grant monies, renewed neighborhood pride, and community action helped steer improvements including new play equipment. (Courtesy TPL.)

Charles B. Wright (1822–1898), president of the Tacoma Land Company, encouraged the company to donate 25 acres of land to the City of Tacoma in 1886. In his honor, the park was named Wright Park. The donation stipulated that within four years the city was to clear the property of debris, seed the land with grass, and plant not less than 150 ornamental shade trees.

By 1892, the land was cleared and trails established in Wright Park. The small statue on the island in the lake, the *Fisherman's Daughter*, is believed to be a gift from Clinton Ferry to the city. In this view, looking north toward Division Avenue, the ornate building to the extreme left is the original Annie Wright Seminary. The school was demolished in 1924 following construction of a new school. (Courtesy WSHS.)

Clinton Ferry donated the two maiden statues at the Division Avenue entrance to Wright Park in 1891. They are replicas of works by Antonio Canova. Ferry purchased these and other statuary for city parks during a trip to Europe in 1889. They are affectionately named "Annie" and "Fannie" for Charles Wright's daughter, Annie, and the namsake of the Fannie Paddock Hospital, now Tacoma General Hospital. (Courtesy TPL.)

The two majestic lions on the Sixth Avenue side of Wright Park were also gifts of Clinton Ferry in 1891. When the park first opened in 1890, Yakima Avenue continued through the park to Division Avenue, as illustrated here. By the early 1920s, the park district began closing the road on weekends. In the interest of public safety, it was permanently closed to vehicular traffic in the late 1920s.

Prior to the Tacoma Land Company's donation of the Wright Park property to the city in 1886, several lots in the southwest corner of the property had already been sold to private individuals. In this view of Wright Park looking from Sixth Avenue toward Division Avenue, those lots with homes built on them can be seen on the left. The city purchased the homes in 1905 and tore them down, bringing Wright Park up to its present size of 29 acres. If one looks closely at the sidewalks on either side of Sixth Avenue, early wooden sidewalks can still be seen. In the distance, elegant new homes rise along South G Street and beyond. (Courtesy WSHS.)

Wright Park's lions have been used as the backdrop for photographs for over 100 years. On April 8, 1940, Bettegene Terry (left), Mary Cathern Terry (center), and Chuck Grisell pose with the two bicycles that were to be given away as the top prizes in the *Tacoma Times*/Borden Elsie cartoon contest. (Courtesy TPL.)

In 1899, the school children of Tacoma, the Sons and Daughters of the American Revolution, and the park commissioners raised money to erect a memorial fountain honoring pioneer Narcissa Whitman in Wright Park. The bronzed iron drinking fountain was manufactured in New York at the cost of $400. The maiden portrayed in the statue atop the fountain holds a water jar on her hip. (Courtesy WSHS.)

By the time these young men came to visit the park in the 1920s, the pond surrounding the *Fisherman's Daughter* statue was beautifully landscaped. The park district had obviously lived up to its original commitment to plant 150 ornamental trees and shrubs in the park. Feeding the swans and sailing small homemade sailboats were both popular activities in this area of Wright Park.

The rustic bridge over Wright Park's pond can be seen in photographs spanning the decades; winter scenes, however, add to the sense of peace and calm in the park. Many Tacoma residents remember days when the winters were so cold that the pond froze solid and filled with ice-skaters.

This very large hollow cedar tree stump was used as a bandstand and playhouse in Wright Park for several years. The stump was part of a display at the Alaska Yukon Pacific Exposition held in Seattle in 1909. Shortly thereafter, it was relocated to Wright Park, where it stood as the central feature of many civic events, concerts, and children's programs until the 1930s.

When park board commissioner George Browne traveled to England in 1890 and returned with a freight car full of trees from the Royal Botanical Gardens of Kew, Wright Park started on its path as the city's arboretum. Here students from Grant Elementary dedicate a buckeye chestnut tree on April, 27, 1922, in honor the 100th anniversary of the birth of Pres. Ulysses S. Grant.

In 1907, William Wolcott Seymour donated $10,000 to the city "to be used as deemed most advisable in beautifying the city." These funds were turned over to the park board, who voted that it be used for building a botanical conservatory in Wright Park. Construction of the conservatory's 12-sided rotunda, two major wings, and entry wing began in February 1908. The W. W. Seymour Botanical Conservatory opened on November 14.

The interior of the conservatory is seen here in 1948 massed with Easter lilies, tulips, and hyacinths for a spring display. The background foliage of banana trees and date palms add to the year-round lushness of revolving exhibits. The plight of the banana tree in Point Defiance Park's greenhouse may have inspired gardener Ebenezer Roberts to support and encourage this display conservatory in Wright Park. (Courtesy TPL.)

Native son and historian Murray Morgan (1916–2000) described the gulch constituting the bulk of Puget Park as the one "that Allen Mason bridged to open the North End to residential development." Allen C. Mason (1855–1920), a Tacoma real estate agent extraordinaire, donated parcels of this steeply wooded ravine to the public for park purposes in 1888, creating Puget Park. Mason also built the first bridge spanning the park's gulch in 1889. In 1919, newspaper accounts record that the Metropolitan Park District briefly entertained a proposal to rename this property Memorial Park in honor of Tacoma boys lost in World War I. More than 50 oak trees and stone markers were planned as a memorial for each life lost, but Memorial Park never came to pass. Proctor Street is the main thoroughfare bridging Puget Park in this 1963 aerial. (Courtesy TPL.)

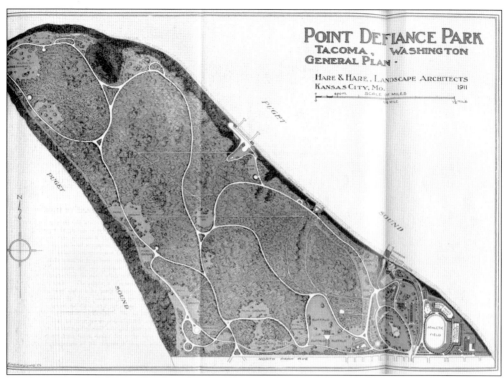

POINT DEFIANCE PARK
TACOMA,   WASHINGTON
GENERAL PLAN ·

HARE & HARE, LANDSCAPE ARCHITECTS
KANSAS CITY, MO.   1911

The Board of Park Commissioners engaged the services of Hare and Hare, a prominent Kansas City, Missouri, landscape architectural firm, in 1910 to create first formal plan for Point Defiance Park. Hare and Hare spent two weeks in March 1911 hiking the park's acreage and taking measurements and photographs. This map was part of the full plan they presented to the park board in July 1911.

Tacoma's U.S. Representative Francis W. Cushman (1867–1909) spearheaded the city's effort to gain title to Point Defiance Park; Pres. Theodore Roosevelt signed the legislation on March 3, 1905. After Cushman's untimely death in office, his family commissioned the memorial statue, dedicated in 1925, that stands near Point Defiance Park's entrance. Its inscription reads, "A noble life, a noble death; Man can ask, God gives no more."

One of the earliest improvements in Point Defiance Park was the construction of a log bridge in 1892 designed by park board secretary F. I. Mead. This bridge was the gateway from the developed areas located closer to the entrance of the park to the wild, forested areas out towards the point. It bridged a gulch, and a stream underneath was dammed to create a pond, which in turn was crossed by a series of smaller picturesque rustic bridges. This area became known as Lovers Lane. The Rustic Bridge, made up of some 3,500 logs, was 250 feet in length and 80 feet high and a major attraction in Point Defiance Park. Frequently pictured in postcards of the era, the bridge was replaced by fill and a paved roadbed in 1933–1934. (Courtesy MPT and Eric Swanson.)

The Pearl Street entrance to Point Defiance Park was framed by a giant log arch designed and built in 1906 by superintendent of parks Ebenezer Rhys Roberts and visible toward the right in the photograph. A newspaper article of the day heralded the structure as "likely to become as famed as the rustic bridge." This impressive entry arch appeared in a number of early views of the park, but it was short-lived and evidently gone by 1911, as there is no mention of it as an existing feature in the Hare and Hare plan written that year. Other structures detailed in this view include the smelter smokestack, a lone house where the town of Ruston now stands, and a variety of fountains in the park's pond.

The Board of Park Commissioners approved $2,220 to build a residence in Point Defiance Park in 1898 for Superintendent Ebenezer Rhys Roberts, referred to as the Keeper's Lodge. Designed by noted Tacoma architect C. A. Darmer, the residence permitted Roberts and his family to live in the park, where he could more easily tend the gardens, feed the zoo animals, and provide general park security. An early newspaper description of the house referred to it as "an ideal rural home, built of polished peeled logs, with an immense colonial veranda running around the entire house." The lodge served as the residence of park superintendents and later executive directors of the Metropolitan Park District until 1980, when it began its present role as a gracious wedding, party, and meeting rental property. (Courtesy C. A. Darmer, grandson of the original architect.)

The Board of Park Commissioners hired Ebenezer Rhys Roberts (1854–1918) in 1890 to begin planting both Wright Park and Point Defiance Park. Roberts was a noted Welsh landscape gardener who had worked in Britain at several large and well-known estates. He immigrated to the United States as a young man and began a career that ultimately included appointment as Tacoma's superintendent of parks. (Courtesy Jean Insel Robeson, Roberts's granddaughter.)

Ebenezer Rhys Roberts and his wife, Mary Ann, had four young children who grew up in the lodge with the wilds of Point Defiance as their backyard. Roberts was such a devoted gardener that he gave three of his four children botanical names. Photographed on the lawn near the lodge c. 1906 are, from left to right, Woodland, Reseda, and Trillium; the eldest, Ebenezer Jr., is not pictured. (Courtesy Jean Insel Robeson, Trillium's daughter.)

Young ladies bicycle past the Point Defiance Park greenhouse around 1915. Built in 1901 between the Keeper's Lodge and the location of today's Rose Garden, the structure was 25 by 100 feet and cost over $2,000 to construct. An additional wing later expanded the square footage for the requirements of serving as both a production greenhouse for plant propagation and as a conservatory for exotic plants and palms. By the early 1920s, the Point Defiance greenhouse functions were moved to newer structures in the southeastern acreage of the park, and the Metropolitan Park District dismantled the commanding edifice. By that time, the W. W. Seymour Conservatory in Wright Park, built in 1908, had taken over as the indoor botanical showplace of Tacoma. (Courtesy WSHS.)

Early visitors to Point Defiance Park enjoyed the lawns, gardens, and arbors so carefully planned and tended by Superintendent Ebenezer Roberts and his able team of gardeners. A pleasing reflection in a lily pond captured the attention of young George Sekor, pictured second from left *c.* 1902, dressed in the Sunday best of young boys of his era. (Courtesy Bonnie Magill.)

Two unidentified park visitors strolled among the plants under cultivation in the Point Defiance Park greenhouse *c.* 1910, admiring the green thumb of park gardeners. Since the structure served as both a working greenhouse as well as an exhibit for tourists, it became increasingly difficult to manage both functions in the same space, even with an addition to the building. (Courtesy THS.)

Dressed for a sunny summer outing, visitors to Point Defiance Park's early zoological collections in the 1890s admire the monkeys in their shelter. The sign on the shed reads: "The people are requested not to torment the animals." Other animal collections in the park included pens of elk, deer, and bison, as well as exotic peacocks and kangaroos. (Courtesy WSHS.)

Polar bears were also early residents of the Point Defiance Park zoological collection. The original bear pits, built in 1899 and 1905, as well as the animal house of 1905 and the deer and elk pens, occupied the start of the uphill slope across from today's Rose Garden. The early animal collection was very much a part of the entry bowl, greenhouse, and formal gardens area. (Courtesy Eric Swanson.)

The Nereides Baths was Tacoma's first indoor swimming pool, located on the bluff overlooking today's Point Defiance Park ferry landing. The name Nereides referred to sea goddesses in Greek mythology who gave aid to sailors. Designed by noted Tacoma architect Frederick Heath, the Nereides Baths opened on Memorial Day 1906. Swimmers enjoyed a 50-by-150-foot pool with water pumped up from Puget Sound and heated to 80 degrees, a diving board, spectators' gallery, dressing rooms, and rented bathing suits. Originally planned as a year-round amenity, the Nereides Baths soon became a summertime-only attraction, providing many seasons of heated saltwater swimming enjoyment. Over time, however, the combination of an aging wooden building exposed to humid saltwater and changing water sanitation regulations numbered the days of the Nereides Baths, and it was demolished in the 1930s. (Courtesy MPT and John Lisicich.)

In November 1898, the Board of Park Commissioners petitioned the U.S. secretary of war for a relic from the USS *Maine*, sunk in Havana Harbor earlier that year, an event that launched the Spanish-American War. Finally a shell was obtained and installed on a base with a commemorative bronze tablet at a grand unveiling on Memorial Day 1913, near the site of today's Japanese Garden. (Courtesy WSHS.)

Transportation from Tacoma out to Point Defiance Park in the era before roads were developed or private cars were common was either by boat or by streetcar. The streetcar line to the park opened with great ceremony on March 1, 1890; the station in Point Defiance Park consisted of this simple rustic shelter situated where the Pagoda building stands today. (Courtesy Jean Insel Robeson.)

CAR STATION FROM KEEPER'S LODGE
PT. DEFIANCE PARK, TACOMA

Built in 1914 in an eclectic oriental temple style and initially referred to as simply "the Car Station," the Pagoda replaced the previous rustic shelter and served as a waiting room for the streetcars, with restrooms and first aid facilities on the lower level. At its opening, the modern and luxurious amenities also included easy chairs, couches, and, in the summer season, an attendant to hand out towels in the ladies' restroom. Men visiting the Pagoda enjoyed a separate smoking room and marble lavatories. The waiting room itself was spacious, with tile floors and walls, comfortable chairs, and a fireplace to keep warm in the cooler weather. The Pagoda became the park's bus station when buses replaced streetcars across Tacoma in 1938; later still, it served as a locale for garden clubs and floral displays. (Courtesy MPT and Eric Swanson.)

INTERIOR OF STATION
POINT DEFIANCE PARK,
TACOMA - 88

The Board of Park Commissioners awarded Edwin Ferris a contract for food and boat rental at Point Defiance Park in 1901. In 1902, the board and Ferris agreed that he could build a restaurant and pavilion at his own expense in exchange for a 10-year contract to operate refreshment and boat-rental concessions at the park. Ferris then built an imposing octagonal structure with a covered porch. The Pavilion, as it became known, contained a restaurant and stands for soft drinks, ice cream, and peanuts; the upper floor served as the Ferrises' residence. This popular amenity became a major draw to Point Defiance Park. Crowds in 1903 were so great that the railway added an additional track on the Point Defiance line to accommodate the increasing throng of visitors to the park. (Courtesy Robin Paterson and Harry Johnson.)

Edwin Ferris's 1903 Pavilion was the only major structure on the waterfront until 1919, when work began on an adjacent structure designed by Tacoma architect Ambrose J. Russell. Completed in two stages—the ground floor in 1921 and the second and third levels in 1925—this second pavilion was a massive concrete building 90 by 170 feet that featured restaurant facilities, a ballroom, and an esplanade. In 1936, the ground floor was converted to use as an aquarium, a popular attraction that moved up the hill in 1963 to more spacious new aquarium facilities at the Point Defiance Zoo. By the late 1930s, the 1903 octagonal Pavilion had seen better days, and it was replaced in 1940 by the Point Defiance Boathouse, built by work crews of the Works Progress Administration (WPA). (Courtesy TPL and MPT.)

In early days, a walk along the Point Defiance beach between the Pavilion and "Picnic Beach" (formally named Owen Beach in 1959) meant long skirts at low tide; nevertheless, two unidentified park visitors managed tree-climbing as well c. 1905. Construction of the raised Promenade along the shore began in 1916, and continued at the rate of 600 feet per year over five years until completion of a 3,000-foot-long seawall. (Courtesy THS.)

Arnold Hansen, Stadium High School class of 1941, president of the Stadium High School Fishing Club, and proud member of the Tacoma Poggie Club, poses with another fine catch in front of the 1940 Point Defiance Boathouse. The boathouse was destroyed by arson in September 1984, leaving decades of memories with those who spent years fishing the waters off Point Defiance. (Courtesy Arnold Hansen.)

In 1934, the Young Men's Business Club of Tacoma started the restoration of Fort Nisqually in Point Defiance Park with the relocation of its two remaining 1850s structures from their original site near DuPont. The Granary, the Factor's House, and a reconstructed bastion were already in place when this photograph captured the reconstruction of the Trade Store. The Civilian Conservation Corps (CCC) and the WPA also worked on the project. (Courtesy TPL.)

The Young Men's Business Club, in conjunction with the Metropolitan Park District, held dedication ceremonies on Labor Day 1934 marking completion of the first phase of the restoration of Fort Nisqually in Point Defiance Park. At the time, only the front palisade wall, pictured in the photograph, was standing; the remainder of the site was unenclosed and contained only the first few structures. (Courtesy TPL.)

During the Depression, work crews funded by federal relief agencies such as the CCC and the WPA were at work in Point Defiance Park. The CCC Camp Point Defiance, housing some 200 workers, stood in 1934 on a bluff below Fort Nisqually; this view over the rooftops looks down the Narrows towards the site of the future Narrows Bridge. (Courtesy TPL.)

The young men of CCC Company 935 at Camp Point Defiance join in song in their barracks after a day of brush clearing and trail building in the park in 1934. The camp opened in the autumn of 1934 and served as a winter camp. CCC members were between the ages of 18 and 25 and made $30 per month, $25 of which was sent to their families. (Courtesy TPL.)

Young men enjoy an evening on the Dodgem bumper cars, one of many ride attractions at Point Defiance Park's Funland. The amusement grounds opened on May 30, 1933, providing an escape from hard times and worries during the Depression and World War II. Residents of the neighborhood still recall the mechanical sounds of the rides and the shrieks of laughter emanating from the park on warm summer nights. (Courtesy WSHS.)

The large wooden swings that dotted the landscape of Point Defiance Park from the 1920s through the 1960s were a very popular feature, and delighted children and adults alike. Sheree Hiller and her brother, Gary, enjoy a ride on a visit to Point Defiance Park about 1959. (Courtesy Sheree Hiller Trefry.)

SUNDAY AFTERNOONS

Take an AUTOMOBILE RIDE over the BEAUTIFUL 5 MILE DRIVE AROUND THE PARK

Start From the Water Tank

Fare 10c   Park Commissioners

At the turn of the 20th century, the vast majority of visitors to Point Defiance Park arrived by boat or streetcar. Even if they motored out, primitive road conditions and limited car ownership kept many visitors from appreciating the outer reaches of Point Defiance Park. Realizing this, the Board of Park Commissioners implemented an early shuttle service through the park in 1915, starting from the Water Tank, which stood near the Lodge. Park visitors paid 10¢ for car passenger service that ran at regular intervals from the Water Tank around Five Mile Drive and back. Some 5,000 visitors patronized this service that first season, more than covering the board's cost of providing it. Perhaps somehow sensing the private-car ownership trend of the future, that same year of 1915, the board authorized construction of the park's first "auto parking ground."

When R. F. Radebaugh purchased 80 acres of land around Wapato Lake in 1881 and built a small cottage, he was hoping for the growth of Tacoma's south end, seen in this aerial photograph. At that time, there were only two families living between his Wapato home and his workplace in downtown Tacoma. He eventually purchased an additional 280 acres around the lake for real estate development. (Courtesy TPL.)

Radebaugh planned to build a fashionable residence district around Wapato Lake. He platted the land, sold large tracts, and built the Fern Hill streetcar line to the lake. In 1888, he hired landscape gardener Ebenezer Roberts to oversee the development of Wapato Lake Park. Roberts's "artistic sense and boundless enthusiasm soon began to make a floral fairyland of the place," according to a newspaper account of the day. (Courtesy WSHS.)

An 1889 advertisement in the *Tacoma Ledger* invited people to Wapato Lake Park for boating, bathing, using a fine pavilion with dancing platform, and more. "All well-disposed people" were welcome to enjoy the pleasures of the park without charge. "All well conducted parties" were to be made welcome. On July 4, 1889, the Tacoma and Fern Hill Railroad sold over 600 tickets each way to Wapato Lake. (Courtesy WSHS.)

This bathing house containing several large dressing rooms for bathers was added in 1889. Other amenities included a refreshment stand, diving spring board, a large bathing raft, and beautiful bridle paths. Glowing reports about the wonderful resort at Wapato Lake stopped appearing in 1891. The nationwide depression hit those invested in railroads especially hard. Radebaugh suffered extreme financial losses during the period and gave up developing the park. (Courtesy WSHS.)

Even though Wapato Lake was no longer being managed as a resort after 1891, the citizens of South Tacoma continued to enjoy the pleasures of the lake, whether it be swimming and boating during summer months or ice-skating on the frozen waters of the lake during the winter, as seen in this picture *c.* 1917. (Courtesy of Harry Johnson.)

Shortly after the establishment of the park district, South Tacoma residents asked that Wapato be incorporated into the growing park system, but funding was not available to purchase lakefront property. Their wish began to come true in 1920, when Horace and Helen Scott donated 20 acres around the lake to the park district. By 1935, the park district owned 62 acres around the lake.

Throughout the 1920s, the park district purchased additional pieces of property and worked to develop Wapato Park. Rowboats were transferred from Point Defiance Park to the lake for people to enjoy, and plans developed to build new dressing rooms, a store, and a boathouse. As the favorite local swimming hole for many South Tacoma residents, it was important to develop the waterfront aspects of the park first. As can be seen in both photographs, a 10-foot diving platform was built for swimmers and swim meets. A shorefront bathhouse can be seen in the bottom image for people to change in and out of their swimming suits.

Along with swimming and boating, children's fishing tournaments have a long tradition at Wapato Lake. In 1947, the park district stocked the lake with 30,000 fingerling trout. Two years later, in 1949, the Tacoma Sportsmen's Club sponsored the first fishing derby on the lake for children. It was not long before the old fishing pier was deemed inadequate, so in 1954, the park district partnered with the Tacoma Sportsmen's Club Auxiliary to fund the construction of a new fishing float large enough to hold 250 young people. In the top photograph, the roof of the 1930s boathouse built by the WPA can be seen. The young man in the bottom image does not seem very happy with his day's catch.

This aerial photograph of Lincoln Park, taken in 1961, illustrates the scale and significance of this park to the southern part of town. The park's origins date to 1889, when the Tacoma Land Company donated 40 acres of land to the city for use as a park. Originally known as South Park, the park commissioners changed the name to Lincoln Park in 1901 to honor Pres. Abraham Lincoln. (Courtesy TPL.)

Lincoln Park originally included the land where Lincoln High School now sits and a deep gulch where the Lincoln Bowl is located. On April 12, 1903, it was described by the *Tacoma Sunday Ledger* as "one of the most picturesque ravines in the West" with "winding paths down deep gulches crossed by rustic bridges, nooks, and resting places along the way, beautiful green terraces, knolls covered with flowers and retreats for a city full of people." (Courtesy Eric Swanson.)

As in other Tacoma parks, park superintendent Roberts was commended for his work at Lincoln Park. Improvements to the park lands, as described in the *Tacoma Sunday Ledger*, "are secured by simply giving a pat and a nudge to nature here and there. Everything on the ground is utilized and improved. The rough knolls are covered with ivy or flowers. A rustic bridge is made with two old logs for sills and cedar limbs for rustic sides."

The upper level of the park was also improved. Here a goldfish pond is surrounded by stones relocated from other areas of the park. Lincoln Park has seen many changes since 1889. In 1911, the city turned over 15 acres to the school district to build Lincoln High School and later, in 1940, leased the gulch portion of the park to the school district for the construction of the Lincoln Bowl.

44

To encourage the outdoor theater movement sweeping the country, a stage platform was built in Lincoln Park in 1928. Virginia Greening Nisker shared this childhood memory of the theater program: "We had a play every week and practiced for it every day. It was performed in a little natural theater using the gulch where the stage was placed down the gully about 100 feet and rows of terraces provided the seating for the audiences. The plays were held on Friday evenings. We usually had quite an audience since there were so many young participants and all of the parents were the appreciative audience."

From its very beginning, Lincoln Park was seen as a place for children to play. Open grassy areas were provided for ball grounds, swings, and other sports. By 1928, swings, slides, sandboxes, and wading pools were available for tots. Here Isabell Finn (left), followed by a smiling Ruth Hagemeier (center) and a very wet James Paul Hanse, runs through the sprinklers to cool off on a hot summer day.

Girl Scout Day Camp was held three days a week at Puget and Lincoln Parks in 1938. The campers pictured here from left to right—Jean Coulter, Carol Betts, Dorothy Spence, Patricia Mozle, Jacqueline Baker, and Patricia Atchison—take a break for refreshments at the camp kitchen in Lincoln Park. The most popular activities were crafts, dramatics, and archery. (Courtesy TPL.)

Fireman's Park has been a fixture of downtown since Tacoma began making improvements c. 1890 to this bluff bounded by A Street and Cliff Avenue between South Eighth and Ninth Streets. At that time, landscape gardener Ebenezer Roberts planted elm seedlings along A Street for the park's beautification. Fireman's Park takes its name from Engine House No. 6, built by the city in 1891 at the southern edge of the original acreage. The park's boundaries have altered considerably over the decades, as the original Cliff Avenue gave way to the new contours of Schuster Parkway in the 1970s. The totem pole, carved in 1903 on commission by wealthy Tacoma businessmen, stood for decades near South Tenth and A Streets; it was moved to Fireman's Park in 1953 and restored there in 1976 with the dedication of the new park.

On April 11, 1901, the Tacoma Land Company donated 22 acres of land on the east side of the city to be "perpetually used and enjoyed as a public park." Landscape gardener Ebenezer Roberts oversaw the early development of McKinley Park. Crews were set to work building footpaths and bridle trails throughout the park interspersed with flowerbeds, rustic seating, and large wood flower vases for all to enjoy. (Courtesy THS.)

Credit for the park's name goes to Martin Hoveland, foreman of the crew working in the park on September 15, 1901, one day after President McKinley's death. Hoveland told the men working for him that from that day on the park would be known as McKinley. Stones spelling out the name of the park were painted white so that the name was plainly visible from boats and trains entering the city.

The Rose Arbor in
McKinley Park,
Tacoma, U. S. A.

Photo by
F. H. Nowell.

As with all the parks under Roberts's management, roses were planted in great quantities. A 1903 article in the *Tacoma Sunday Ledger* notes, "But in this park, as in the others, nature is being reinforced by art. . . . Every natural object that is beautiful and decorative is spared and improved. . . . The common trees are thinned out, the beautiful dogwood, and the rarer varieties remain untouched. Everywhere there are fine little effects."

A distinctive feature of McKinley Park is a natural spring along the upper edge of the park. Roberts turned this to good use. Near the street, he fashioned a large lily pond and on the hillside built a concrete wall to contain the water and provide a swimming pool for boys and girls to enjoy on hot summer days.

As the playground movement gained momentum in the 1920s, improvements at McKinley Park included a wading pool, comfort station (restroom), recreation building, volleyball courts, and playground equipment in the park's lower level. McKinley Park's playground program grew in popularity over the years. Attendance for the summer of 1937 was 20,549. Unfortunately, by the 1950s, the park's lower levels were not heavily used, and the equipment and facilities were removed.

As can be attested to by this photograph from 1928, the people from neighborhoods surrounding McKinley Park were active participants in the many recreational programs offered at the park. A significant impact on the accessibility of this park came in 1962 with the beginning of construction of Interstate Highway 5, or the Tacoma Freeway, along the northern borders of the park, effectively walling off McKinley from the city.

South Park was originally part of the Spanaway Lake and Flume Line right-of-way for the Tacoma Light and Water Company, a private water system. In 1893, the City of Tacoma purchased the water system in order to provide more reliable service. Shortly thereafter, the city abandoned the inadequate lines and built a new water system. In February 1905, the city set aside the old right-of-way as a park and parkway.

By 1915, the annual report of the Metropolitan Park District noted that "the beds of flowers and bulbs in South Park bloomed as gaily as usual" and that South Park was becoming each year more popular for local picnics. The report recommended building a comfort station as soon as practicable in 1916. (Courtesy Eric Swanson.)

In 1941, the U.S. Army was looking for sites in Tacoma for the construction of United Service Organizations (USO) facilities. The park district leased a portion of South Park to the army for this purpose. The facility consisted of a snack bar, kitchen, clubroom, library, hobby workshop, and 3,000-square-foot auditorium. The USO closed in late 1944, and the park district took over management of the facility as a community center.

Wilma E. Lewis, photographed standing next to a water fountain installed at South Park in 1928, was the director of the South Tacoma USO. One of Miss Lewis's jobs was to oversee the Junior Hostess Club. According to the club's bylaws, unmarried girls from 18 to 35 were eligible to apply to serve the "spiritual, educational and recreational needs of the men and women of the Armed Forces." (Courtesy Dorothy Lowe.)

Relaxing in front of the South Park USO in May 1944 are, from left to right, Bill Brannon, Dot Lowe, Ken Awsumb, and Amy Chandler. There were strict codes of conduct at the USO. Junior hostesses were not allowed to wear slacks unless leaving or returning from hayrides, cruises, or other outside events. No bobby socks were allowed except for special events. Stockings or leg make-up was preferable in the building. (Courtesy Dorothy Lowe.)

As a USO facility, the South Park Center's 3,000-square-foot auditorium was a popular location for dances. When the park district purchased the building, regular community dances continued to be a popular part of the recreational programming, as evidenced by this dance class for teens. (Courtesy TPL.)

In 1947, the South Tacoma Community Center, as it was known then, celebrated its third anniversary as a community recreation building by offering a varied program of craft classes for adults, drama and dancing classes for youngsters, athletic programs for grade-school boys, and teen and adult social groups. The pottery class, shown here, was especially popular. Shortly thereafter, the South Park Craft Guild was formed.

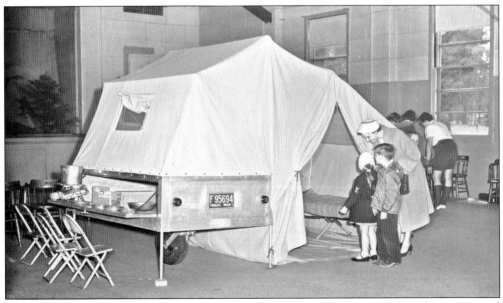

South Park's large auditorium was frequently utilized for community events, such as this commercial trailer exhibit during the Outdoor Living Institute held at the center in 1960. The wooden floors, so conducive to dancing, were covered to protect them from any damage during the event.

Dancing is a theme running through the programming at South Park from its earliest days. The wood floors are perfect for dance of all types. Classes have included ballet, tap, modern dance, tumbling, baton twirling, and more. Dances for seniors were introduced into the program soon after the park district began managing the building, and they continue today. A separate room was later dedicated to ballet instruction, with the installation of mirrors on the walls and exercise barres along the walls at heights for dancers of various ages, as illustrated by the young girl getting special attention in proper posture from the ballet instructor.

Another feature of South Park Community Center is the performance stage in the auditorium, making this venue perfect for dancers of all ages to show off what they have learned. Friends and family often filled the auditorium to watch dancers, baton twirlers, actors, singers, musicians, and cheerleaders perform. Above, young tap dancers focus on the steps they have worked so hard to master. Below, Jean Ramsted, on the drum, instructs a 1957 class in modern dance with Joyce Loveland (center) and JoAnn Kerrick.

Two

THE PARK SYSTEM GROWS

Acreage across the city dedicated to park development continued to grow in many ways following the establishment of the Metropolitan Park District of Tacoma in 1907, resulting in the dynamic expansion of the system over the first 100 years of its existence.

Private citizens such as Frank Alling, Benjamin Harvey, George Washington Eldridge, and Leona Maude Kandle donated land or money to purchase property throughout the growing city with the specific intent of providing a safe place for children to play.

The Board of Park Commissioners also strategically purchased open spaces throughout the city to ensure that, as neighborhoods spread further away from that city's core, parkland and recreational opportunities would be available for all. Manitou Park, McKinley Playfield, Oakland Playfield, Jefferson Park, Portland Avenue Playfield, and Garfield Park are just a few examples of these early additions to the park system.

Additionally the board made funds available to purchase developed properties from private parties, such as Titlow Park in 1926 and Meadow Park Golf Course in 1962, to add to the expanding variety of public recreational opportunities for Tacoma's citizenry.

A long-term partner in the development of parks throughout the city is the Tacoma School District. Many parks, such as DeLong Park, Franklin Park, and Harmon Playfield, abut Tacoma School District property and are named for their respective schools.

The citizens of Dash Point and Browns Point, even though residing outside Tacoma city limits, voted to join the Metropolitan Park District's tax base in 1922 to ensure professional stewardship of parklands within their jurisdictions. Cooperative agreements between the Metropolitan Park District, local improvement clubs and other government agencies have added to these Northeast Tacoma waterfront preserves.

The number of Tacoma parks continues to grow. Welcome additions come about thanks to community activism such as Neighbors' Park and Blueberry Park. Others are open space purchased in partnership with numerous organizations and agencies to preserve urban green space and waterfront access. Swan Creek, Ruston Way, and Oak Tree Park all contribute to the variety of parks enjoyed by the people of Tacoma.

Frank Alling (1839–1912) would be pleased to see these children enjoying this 1950 puppet show in the park named in his honor. Alling, an early Tacoma pioneer, donated his six-acre homestead, Alling Fruit Farm, to the city in 1912 to be used for park purposes. Alling's final request was also granted; his ashes were buried at the base of a Lombardy poplar in the park.

Alling Park, located at South Fifty-sixth Street and Sheridan Avenue, received many improvements during the 1930s thanks to the WPA. The wading pool was completed in 1938, and an adjacent ballfield built. Tennis courts that could be flooded and frozen in the winter to allow ice-skating were built in the northeast corner. A picnic shelter is hidden in the trees on the south side of the park.

In 1915, the park district purchased Manitou Park, 10 acres of land in the southern part of the city. The park district wanted to purchase land for park purposes before it became too expensive. As automobile traffic along Pacific Highway—now South Tacoma Way—increased, the park district decided to build a campground on the Manitou property to assist tourists needing overnight accommodations.

The park district installed lights, water, toilets, and bathing and laundry facilities and built large ovens and tables under shelters. Manitou Park was one of the best tourist camps along Pacific Highway. Charging 50¢ per day for camping, it was self-supporting, even if many in 1922 thought it too expensive. By 1923, the records indicate that 11,000 people in 3,086 automobiles camped at Manitou.

Manitou Car Camp closed in 1927, when the park district decided that playground facilities were more important for the growing community of South Tacoma. The park district cleared out all the camping equipment, planted sod, built a wading pool and new ovens, and installed swings. During the summer of 1937, records show that 15,304 children visited the park.

Manitou Park's summer recreation program continues to be popular. These 1955 playground participants proudly display the spaceship they created as a part of the summer playground program. The spaceship is called the "Manitou Star Chaser," and the youngsters hold up signs saying "Mars or Bust" and "Goodby Manitou, Hello Mars."

In 1922, a committee of the Dash Point Improvement Club urged the park board to incorporate the public beach at Dash Point into the park district. Dash Point beach was growing in popularity but was without bathing equipment or facilities. The citizens of Dash Point could vote to join the park district, but only if they could convince the citizens of Browns Point and the tide flats to do the same thing because the territory voting itself to join the park district had to be contiguous to the district's existing boundaries. The adjoining areas agreed, and the vote was favorable for annexation on May 23, 1922. Shortly after Dash Point joined the park district, swimming lessons were offered. In 1927, nearly 500 people were given free swimming lessons in the first week of the session. A second session was quickly scheduled.

In 1911, A. R. Titlow (1858–1923) built the Hesperides Hotel on land in Tacoma's west side. The three-and-one-half story building was designed by Frederick Heath and named in honor of Titlow's daughters. In Greek mythology, the Hesperides were three nymphs who tended a blissful garden in a far western corner of the world. The hotel had 30 guest rooms, a formal dining room, a billiard room, a barbershop, and a ladies' parlor. Following Titlow's death in 1923, the hotel and surrounding property were sold to the park district, which renamed it Titlow Lodge. The lagoon in front of the hotel was a popular swimming hole for many on Tacoma's west side who did not want to venture into the cold waters of Puget Sound on the other side of the hotel.

In the 1930s, it was discovered that Titlow Lodge was sinking into the ground. Instead of tearing down the structure, WPA crews were directed in 1938 to demolish all except the first floor and to rebuild the roof, thus lightening the building's weight. Since that time, the lodge and surrounding 74 acres of parkland have provided the community a lovely waterfront location for picnics, sports, and summer playground programs. Hints of the beautiful, rustic Hesperides Hotel are still evident in the remaining first floor of the lodge, making it a popular spot for weddings and other festive occasions.

Jefferson Park - Showing progress of grading, June 2ⁿᵈ 1933

The view above of Jefferson Park in 1933 shows the park under construction from the corner of North Seventh and Mason Streets looking northeast. Jefferson Park entered the Metropolitan Park District as incremental land purchases beginning in 1922 for the purposes of establishing a park in Tacoma's west end; the name came from its proximity to Jefferson Elementary School. Since the Board of Park Commissioners had little money to turn the overgrown and swampy tract into a park and playground, the neighborhood formed improvement clubs to pitch in with labor and funding. Crews such as the WPA helped finish the grading and construction of a small community building with federal work-relief funding during the 1930s. The opening dedication was held in November 1937. In the photograph below, the Jefferson Park Playground Association helps install lighting in 1949. (Courtesy TPL.)

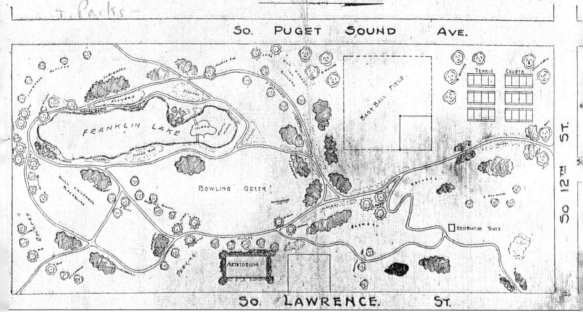

The idea for a park adjacent to Franklin Elementary School dates to 1909, when former mayor and park board commissioner W. W. Seymour donated two lots to the Franklin School that were to be used to "teach the children something of flora culture." Seymour suggested that the lots be used as part of Franklin Park when it should be developed. In 1911, the park board suggested purchasing 12 blocks near Franklin School for a park. The above plan was drawn up by park board president Frederick Heath to illustrate what could "be done with an area already adapted by nature for the making of a veritable beauty spot." The park district was not successful in raising the money for the purchase of the Franklin Park property, so local community groups took the matter into their own hands and began a fund-raising effort.

Covering more than 20 acres between South Twelfth and South Sixteenth Streets, Franklin Park was a gift to the park district from the West End Playground Association in 1937. Community groups worked for 15 years to raise the money for the parkland. Here (left to right) Henry Pitcher, Mrs. J. B. Champlain, C. F. Mason, Sherman Ingels, and Pearl Lee review the plans for the long-awaited park. (Courtesy TPL.)

An early feature of Franklin Park was Hoodlum Lake. Summer-like weather on March 16, 1947, had children, like these boys rafting on Hoodlum Lake, out enjoying the sunshine. From left to right, the boys are Paul Gerber, Daryl Zylstra, Dennis Cook, and Jimmie Cook. Although the lake was drained during the park's development, a wading pool was added in 1949. (Courtesy TPL.)

Nearly 100 women of the Monday Civic Club took part in a tree-planting ceremony at Franklin Park on June 8, 1948. This memory grove was planted as part of the conservation program of the National Federation of Women's Clubs. Approximately 200 fir trees were laid out in a one-acre plot, with each tree bearing the name of a club member or city official. (Courtesy TPL.)

Kandle Playfield was the gift of Leona Maude Kandle, who left a bequest in her will for a playfield to be named for her father, George B. Kandle. The Tacoma School District deeded almost nine acres adjacent to Mont Downing Elementary School, visible in the background, to the Metropolitan Park District. Clearing was under way in the summer of 1960, and the dedication of Kandle Playfield took place in July 1961.

Neighborhood boys of the 1950s found Jane Clark Playfield a good spot to practice building pyramids. The park was made possible by Benjamin L. Harvey, who left his estate in 1933 to the Metropolitan Park District to acquire playground acreage in the North End. Harvey's will further stipulated that the eventual park be named after his mother, Jane Clark. In 1936, the park district bought property bounded by North Thirty-ninth, Ferdinand, and Orchard Streets, but serious work did not begin on park development until 1948. An allocation from a 1952 tax levy supported by the North End Recreation Association funded construction of the recreation building, and the wading pool was a gift from the Downtown Kiwanis Club. Dedication ceremonies in June 1953 formally welcomed Jane Clark Playfield into the growing system of parks across Tacoma.

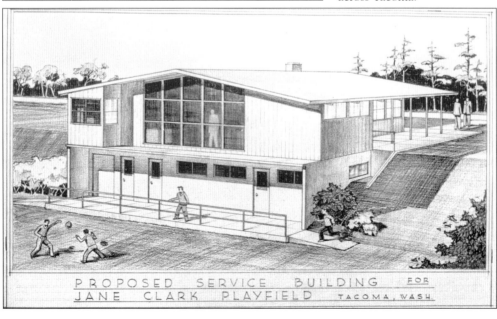

PROPOSED SERVICE BUILDING FOR JANE CLARK PLAYFIELD TACOMA, WASH.

Old Town Tacoma, Old Town Park, and Point Defiance Park shared an intertwined history with the Job Carr Cabin. In 1899, Clinton P. Ferry and the Board of Park Commissioners spearheaded the drive to move the Job Carr Cabin from its original Old Town location to Point Defiance Park as a means of preserving it. By 1900, as seen in the postcard above, the cabin stood near the park's present tennis courts on the bluff above the Vashon Island ferry landing. In 1917, workers moved the cabin to the entrance area of the park's Five Mile Drive, where it resided for decades before its dismantling. The 1976 photograph below recorded the acreage that would become Old Town Park, where the Job Carr Cabin Museum partnered with Metro Parks Tacoma to reconstruct the cabin, once again near its original site.

Acquisition of Swan Creek Park began in 1966. Swan Creek, its canyon, and adjacent land have long been looked upon as a treasure which must be preserved in an urbanizing area. A citizens group called the Swan Creek Conservation and Development Committee formed to help save the property in the early 1960s. Public support grew, and Tacoma voters passed a ballot issue to purchase the initial 152 acres. Now 322 acres in size, Swan Creek's canyon and stream are classified a Fish and Wildlife Conservation Area. The park district maintains the streamside trail and initiated a trail-reconstruction project through the Americorps program. Above, Americorps workers demonstrate log-lifting techniques. Below, crews work to clean up the trails following a 1997 ice storm. (Courtesy Kerry Phibbs.)

Garfield Park entered the system of the Metropolitan Park District, as did several other parks, with the slow acquisition of parcels of land over several years. From 1912 through 1927, the district acquired acreage from the Tacoma Land and Improvement Company and other parties for the express purpose of creating a public park. In 1938, The WPA recorded this outline of Garfield Park, one of its work-relief projects for the Metropolitan Park District during the Depression. Bordered by the venerable Tacoma institutions of the Annie Wright Seminary to the west and the Tacoma Lawn Tennis Club to the southwest, Garfield Park slopes down to a gulch that is part of the Bayside Trails system. The Metropolitan Park District and the Americorps program invested many hours repairing steps and trails along the slopes of the gulch in 1996. (Courtesy Kerry Phibbs.)

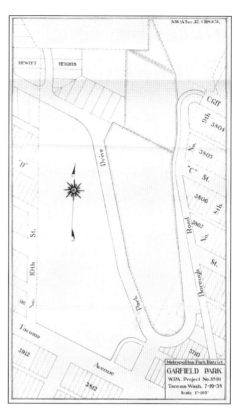

Enthusiastic children perform the ribbon-cutting duties at Neighbors' Park on March 18, 2006. Once a single vacant lot at South Eighth and I Streets in a blighted section of town, community members took charge and worked together to turn it into a valuable resource. This park now contains play equipment, a basketball court, flower gardens, picnic benches, grassy areas, and safe, clean walkways and ramps.

A visitor to Blueberry Park at East Eightieth and D Streets picks delicious blueberries from one of over 4,000 blueberry bushes in the park. In 1994, when the Tacoma School District deeded 23 acres to the park district, this remnant of an old blueberry farm was completely overgrown with blackberry vines and was unusable. Neighbors came together to clear the land and salvage the blueberries to the benefit of everyone.

Three

A VISION OF THE NATURAL WORLD

Three distinct Metropolitan Park District properties span the past century in their unique dedication to conservation: Point Defiance Zoo and Aquarium, the Tacoma Nature Center, and Northwest Trek Wildlife Park.

The Point Defiance Park zoological collection began in the 1890s with herds of elk, deer, and bison; bears, monkeys, lions, kangaroos, and pheasants arrived by 1910. Many found their way to the zoo by boat, brought by sailors from distant exotic ports. The aquarium, established in 1936 on the park's waterfront, remained a separate entity until construction of a new aquarium on zoo grounds in 1963. The Point Defiance Zoo and Aquarium has earned wide acclaim for its evolving animal exhibits and conservation programs and its accreditation by the Association of Zoos and Aquariums (AZA). Since 1979, it has focused on land and marine animals of the Pacific Rim.

The lake of the Tacoma Nature Center at Snake Lake was for centuries a natural wetland. By 1900, though at some distance from the growing young city of Tacoma, it was popular for fishing and ice-skating. The Metropolitan Park District formally acquired the acreage in 1928 with plans to develop a municipal golf course, but the onset of the Depression negated that idea. The lake and its environs lay mostly undeveloped until a 1969 Tahoma Audubon Society proposal to use the area for ecological study. After a great deal of work by concerned citizens, local educational institutions, and government agencies, the Snake Lake Nature Center (original name) opened in 1979 as an oasis of nature surrounded by the city.

Northwest Trek Wildlife Park began in 1971, with the generous donation by Dr. David and Connie Hellyer of more than 500 forested acres near Eatonville to the Metropolitan Park District. The Hellyers wanted to create a park exhibiting North American wildlife in a free-roaming natural environment. After four years of diligent planning and intense fund-raising, Northwest Trek opened to the public in 1975. Since then, additional acreage has further protected the park and provided new opportunities for conservation and natural exhibits. Northwest Trek also proudly maintains AZA accreditation.

This view of feeding time in the deer pen in Point Defiance Park *c*. 1900 illustrates the early fencing and enclosures for the elk and deer herds in the park's zoological collection. Ebenezer Rhys Roberts, the superintendent of Point Defiance Park from the 1890s to 1908, was in charge not only of the park's greenhouse and gardens, but also served as the head animal keeper until 1905.

Additions to the Point Defiance Park zoological collection in the World War I era were two of its first celebrity residents. In 1913, Dave and Dandy, the faithful oxen who pulled Ezra Meeker's wagon in 1906 on a commemorative trip over sections of the Oregon Trail, came to spend their retirement with the deer, elk, and bison herds of Point Defiance Park. Dave and Dandy were local celebrities known even decades later, thanks to taxidermy and their subsequent exhibition hitched to the wagon in the old Washington State Historical Society building. (Courtesy WSHS.)

As this c. 1911 photograph indicates, the zoo once was located lower in Point Defiance Park than its present uphill location. The 1905 animal house, as well as other shelters for the elk and deer herds, occupied the start of the uphill slope across from today's Rose Garden, situating the early animal collection very near the park's entrance, greenhouse, and formal gardens. The Hare and Hare plan of 1911, the first formal master plan for Point Defiance Park, advised that the animal pens be removed from the entry area to make way for lawns and a drive, a suggestion that the Board of Park Commissioners followed. The plan also advocated construction of additional zoo structures, such as a zoological museum and a combined aviary-aquarium in the park entry area, but these proposals were never pursued. The Keeper's Lodge is visible behind the central vault of the greenhouse roof and is the only structure shown in this early view that remains in Point Defiance Park today. The large greenhouse was gone from the park by the 1920s.

Unidentified Tacoma children of the 1930s enjoy an encounter with one of the residents of the Pheasantry, the aviary built in 1914 to house the Point Defiance Zoo's bird collection. The Pheasantry building exhibited the rustic Japanese style of architecture advocated for use in Point Defiance Park by the Hare and Hare plan of 1911; a new aviary building replaced it in 1968. (Courtesy TPL.)

Animal keeper Wilhelm Jordan feeds Dub Dub the harbor seal in 1940. Arguably the most popular aquarium attraction ever at Point Defiance, Dub Dub arrived at three weeks of age in 1938. He astounded the zoo staff by living to the ripe old age of 33. When he died in 1972, Dub Dub had enjoyed more than twice the average life span of harbor seals in the wild. (Courtesy TPL.)

Zoo visitors Marleigh Udall and Jerry Hopper admire Butch and Boots, the zoo's grizzly bears, in the summer of 1950. Built in 1899, the bear pit enclosure was one of the longest-standing structures at the Point Defiance Zoo. Long since vacated, as animal care and exhibits evolved, it was demolished in 2003 to make room for the Wild Wonders Outdoor Theater. (Courtesy TPL.)

In the summer of 1959, Point Defiance Park Zoo expansion and improvements featured the construction and dedication of the Children's Farm Zoo, funded by a special public election, which exhibited cows, chickens, rabbits, ducks, and goats and encouraged their interaction with city children. Care of the farm animals was a cooperative venture between zoo staff and chapters of the Future Farmers of America.

In 1963, the Point Defiance Aquarium moved from the waterfront Pavilion, its home since the 1930s, up the hill and into then-state-of-the-art quarters in its new round building, which still stands on the grounds and today houses the North Pacific Aquarium. This move finally united the land and marine animal collections in one location, and the park's zoological attraction became known as the Point Defiance Zoo and Aquarium.

Curator Jim Short explains the intelligence and behavior of Pacific white-sided dolphins in the Rocky Shores exhibit in the early 1980s. Metropolitan Park District voters passed a 1977 bond issue to invest in Point Defiance Zoo and Aquarium, essentially doubling its size, rebuilding many exhibits, and adding new ones such as the Rocky Shores complex.

This *c.* 1973 aerial view shows the woodland and wetland acreage of the Tacoma Nature Center at Snake Lake. The middle and lower right ovals flanking the reserve are the tracks and athletic fields of Bellarmine Prep and Henry Foss High Schools, respectively. At right, Highway 16 spans the southern end of the reserve; the bridge, newly completed in 1972, was a concession to environmental concerns.

Alf West and his brother fish at the edge of Snake Lake around 1920. The boys' father, Thorkild "Ted" Thorkildson, newly arrived from Norway, built a home at the southeast end of the lake, where the family lived from 1914 to 1922. The posts in the lake in this photograph marked the family's territory out into the water for ice cutting and duck pens. (Courtesy Alf West.)

Robert Ramsey (1920–2006) of the Tahoma Audubon Society, fondly remembered as "the Old Ranger," worked tirelessly through the 1970s to preserve the land and promote nature education on the Snake Lake property the park district had formally acquired in 1928. Ramsey, a landscape architect by profession, became the first manager of the Snake Lake Nature Center when it opened in 1979.

Robert Ramsey served as manager from 1979 to 1987. For several months, he had no building from which to direct operations and educational programs, and consequently he worked out of his Honda station wagon. In September 1980, the Tacoma School District loaned the nature center a portable building; a second portable followed in 1983, providing much needed space. The field lights of Heidelberg Park are visible across Tyler Street.

The Snake Lake Nature Center crafted a subtle name change in the late 1980s, becoming the Tacoma Nature Center. The adjustment in nomenclature countered any negative perception, as the lake's name actually derived from its long shape and not from an overabundance of serpentine inhabitants. As a wetlands preserve, aquatic interpretation and education has been at the forefront of the facility's mission since its inception in 1979, whether from the bridge across Snake Lake or at off-site environmental education programs. In 1988, the Tacoma Nature Center began to offer guided educational walks along Tacoma's west-side Titlow Beach, which added environmental interpretation of Puget Sound to the center's many successful offerings.

David and Constance Hellyer donated some 500 acres near Eatonville to the Metropolitan Park District in1971, with the stipulation that the property become a natural zoo featuring North American game animals. "Doc" Hellyer, a Tacoma pediatrician, purchased the land in the 1930s. He and Constance raised their family in a series of rustic cabins and a home they built on the property. David Hellyer passed away in 2006.

This 1938 view depicts the wilderness that would become Northwest Trek some 40 years later. The acreage included lakes, meadows, stands of Douglas fir, hemlock, cedar, and alder, and swamps created by beaver dams. David and Constance Hellyer wanted to ensure that their land, which they called Horseshoe Ranch, and its wildlife would be preserved as a legacy for future generations to appreciate.

Following the Hellyers' 1971 land donation, voters passed a general obligation bond proposition to help create the wildlife park. Northwest Trek Wildlife Park opened in the summer of 1975 with four propane-powered trams that each pulled two trailers. Here the trams carry visitors past a herd of bison in the free-roaming area. The Hellyers retained lifetime occupancy of their home on Horseshoe Lake within the park.

Northwest Trek animal keepers Ed Cleveland (left), Dick Buchonis (center), and Dave Ellis clip the flight feathers on the wings of a great horned owl to render it flightless, which allowed the park to display the bird in a new non-enclosed, naturalistic exhibit in 1985. Other exhibits opened in subsequent years, featuring outdoor, naturalistic cougar, lynx, bobcat, porcupine, and grizzly and black bear habitats.

Doc Hellyer himself leads a tour of visitors near the entrance of Northwest Trek. Since 1975, over three million people from around the world have visited the park to view the bison galloping across the meadows and the bull elk clashing and to walk the trails of the natural exhibits. The Hellyer Natural History Center, a laboratory/classroom open to students, scientists, and the business community, opened in 2000.

From its early days, Northwest Trek Wildlife Park has offered unique opportunities for learning about nature and conservation in the wild. Alongside programs offering more serious education in research and ecology are purely fun activities to engage park visitors, such as the regional favorite pictured here, slug races.

Four

PICNICS, PLAYGROUNDS, AND PET PARADES

The grand old parks of Tacoma, both large and small, formed the core of civic green spaces at the beginning of the 20th century. Once the parks were planted and cultivated, the people of Tacoma flocked to them for the respite offered by their forests, shores, lawns, and gardens. As Bernice Newell, reporter for the *Tacoma Daily Ledger*, put it in 1903, "[parks] are all the resort the great army of busy people have."

Indeed, in the decades before widespread ownership of automobiles, travel far from home, and extensive opportunities for recreation, Tacoma's parks and their simple pleasures were the destination of choice for several generations. Picnics are one such pleasure that recall good times in favorite Tacoma parks and remain across the decades.

Additionally, from about 1900 through the 1920s, Tacoma realized a growing national sentiment that parks should provide for the wholesome recreation of children and youth. Through the 1920s and beyond, the Metropolitan Park District cooperated with community groups, the Tacoma School District, and private benefactors to add to and augment the more formal parks with supervised playfields. An editorial in the *Tacoma Daily Ledger* proclaimed after the successful 1927 summer: "Tacoma has learned that it pays to take the children off the streets, out of the alleys and to assemble them for play in places where none but the best influences can reach them. Through the adoption of the plan of supervised playgrounds, Tacoma has taken a decided step in the direction of the conservation of its greatest asset the children."

In the following decades, the Metropolitan Park District continued to acquire land for parks and to cooperate with the Tacoma School District in joint-use agreements for recreational opportunities for both children and adults. In 1944, the park and school district boards established the Tacoma Recreation Commission to ensure cohesive programs were available to all sectors of the city. Since the 1960s, the Metropolitan Park District has sponsored Playground Leaders Institute for training those supervising the playfield activities. And throughout the decades, Tacoma's citizens have created beloved memories in these big backyards that belong to all.

Seattle was not the only popular destination in 1909, the year it hosted the Alaska-Yukon-Pacific Exposition, a World's Fair held to publicize the development of the Pacific Northwest. This group of unidentified picnic-goers found that Tacoma's Point Defiance Park made a delightful stop that summer of 1909, when hats, neckties, and even gloves were suitable attire for such outings. The photograph at left shows their arrival in the park, assisted in some unknown fashion by the wooden wheelbarrow—perhaps a heavy picnic basket? The photograph below finds them comfortably situated on the beach, where a close examination of the spread on the tablecloth reveals sandwiches, deviled eggs, and a large can of pork and beans. The gentlemen of the party evidently took turns taking these photographs. (Courtesy MPT and Eric Swanson.)

PICNIC GROUND PT. DEFIANCE PARK, TACOMA WASH.

Large picnic groups flocked to Point Defiance Park's popular picnic grounds for decades. The main area was located on the plateau above the beach, west of the original octagonal pavilion, and was a feature at Point Defiance Park from the early 1900s. The photograph above indicates the popularity of the locale in this era. Additional picnic shelters in the park's forest region were described around 1915 as having fireplaces with 3-foot-by-6-foot concrete stoves and stone chimneys. Note the picnic stove at the left edge of the image above that matches this description. The photograph below shows a close-up view of this same cooking stove, where a woman with pushed-up sleeves manages several pots and kettles.

STOVE IN PICNIC GROUND. POINT DEFIANCE PARK ~47

Metropolitan Park District of Tacoma staff gather for a group photograph in the 1920s on the steps of the Northern Pacific building, at South Seventh Street and Pacific Avenue. Known then as the City Hall Annex, it housed the park district offices. Unfortunately staff members in this photograph remain unidentified as of this publication; Metro Parks Tacoma would appreciate assistance with identification if community members can supply names.

Isabelle Havel, general supervisor of playgrounds, and Tom Lantz, superintendent of public recreation, give a presentation on Metropolitan Park District policies to trainees in the Playground Leaders Institute of 1961. The posters on the wall welcome the new leaders to the training and detail winning ways to work with children. Other topics on the week's agenda included how to direct playground pet shows and playfield circuses.

Isabelle Havel (front row, far right, c. 1965) formalized the training of playfield supervisors with creation of the Playground Leaders Institute. Havel, who started work in the playgrounds as "the puppet lady" around 1950, later worked full-time for the Metropolitan Park District and established many landmark recreation programs, crafted with great ingenuity in the early days, when funding was scarce.

The Central Playfield was established in the summer of 1927 on the grounds of the old Central School at South Eleventh and G Streets (today the site of Bates Technical College), with the goal of serving children across a wide section of the city. The playfield, a city block square, was terraced to accommodate the hillside terrain and featured supervised playground equipment, sport fields, and tennis courts. Eva Davis, a 1926 Stadium High School graduate, was one of the first playground directors. Employed by the new recreation department of the Metropolitan Park District, she was assigned to Central Playfield to supervise daily activities; later in life, she would serve over 20 years on the Board of Park Commissioners.

The recreation movement, which spread across the county in the early 20th century, emphasized not only the development of playfields and programs in parks, but also encouraged private citizens to develop healthy outdoor play equipment to add to their own backyards. These unidentified children in the backyard of 3404 North Twenty-fifth Street were probably the envy of the neighborhood.

In a timeless, ideal image of American boyhood, Owen Dickson, aged seven and accompanied by his faithful dog Coachie, traces a picture as part of a summer crafts program at McKinley Playfield in August 1936. Sponsored by the Metropolitan Park District, activities also included sewing and other handicraft hobbies. (Courtesy TPL.)

In August 1936, Wright Park boasted a new 12-foot-square concrete checkerboard at the north end of the park. The checkerboard was black and white, with yellow and red checkers; players moved them with a stick, through a loop on each checker. Sizeable crowds assembled to watch National Checker Champion Willie Ryan (in the suit) take on local players in exhibition games. (Courtesy TPL.)

A confident man and two rather more hesitant boys, all unidentified, take to the parallel bars in the playground at Wright Park in 1959. The playground in the park used to border the edges of South Yakima Avenue, which originally cut straight through the length of Wright Park. The avenue was closed to traffic and the street replaced by a lawn and playground in the 1930s.

Elaborate May Day festivities were popular annual events in Wright Park in the 1920s. This unidentified queen of May Day 1927 presides from a flower-festooned throne over a court that features many attendants, including one dressed as Robin Hood. These festivities also included groups of children dancing around maypoles and sizeable crowds of appreciative onlookers.

These proud young Tacoma children pose with their winning entries in the Flower Show of 1940; the location of the specific park is not recorded. In a community still dealing with the effects of the Depression and soon to be facing the limitations of the home front during World War II, Tacomans made fun out of simple things readily at hand, such as flowers from their backyards.

Young women play "captain ball" on the expansive lawn of Jefferson Park in 1940. This view to the north shows the field house in the background, which opened in 1937 as a neighborhood center for classes, dances, and recreation in Tacoma's burgeoning residential west end. The chalk squares and circles marking the boundaries of the game are visible on the grass.

Jefferson Park featured a wide variety of fun day-camp activities in the summer of 1955. Under the direction of playground leaders Janet Brinkman and Dan Inveen, two unidentified day campers point to the Hat Day theme, "If you have a head, you can wear a hat." Other activities advertised were a checker tournament, swim lessons, and Howdy Doody Week.

In August 1947, Harry Bailey proudly accepted a certificate as having the most freckles in the annual city-wide Freckles Contest at McKinley Playfield, a testament that a kid could have big fun without lots of fancy equipment or toys. Other categories in the contest included biggest, smallest, lightest, and darkest freckles.

Metropolitan Park District leaders and neighborhood volunteers assist children with crafts at McCarver Playfield in 1960 and work on getting out the juvenile vote at the same time. The sign on the wall behind them reads, "If you want a good playground next summer, tell your parents to vote YES to parks & playgrounds Sept 13th."

Popular outdoor spots for picnics included Titlow Beach and American Lake Park. The photograph above shows two gentlemen identified only as "Daddy" and "Uncle Elmer" relaxing on Titlow Beach on July 4, 1915. At that time, Titlow Beach boasted the private Hotel Hesperides, built in 1911 by Tacoma lawyer Aaron Titlow as a waterfront resort. After Titlow's death in 1923, the Metropolitan Park District bought the property, and the hotel eventually became the Titlow Lodge Community Center. The photograph below pictures the Johnson family of Cedar Street in Tacoma dining alfresco at American Lake Park in 1912. The Metropolitan Park District acquired this park in parcels between 1914 and 1936; it became part of Pierce County in early 1959, when the county created its own department of parks and recreation. (Both courtesy TPL.)

"Putt" and Bessie Mossman, a brother-and-sister team of champion horseshoe pitchers from Des Moines, Iowa, traveled the Northwest in the summer of 1931 for tournament and exhibition matches, some of which were held in Tacoma's Point Defiance Park. At the tournament picnic, Putt (second from left) holds his birthday cake at tables laden with picnic fare and flowers; his sister Bessie stands on his left. (Courtesy Jan and Vennard Lahti.)

Picnics were popular and casual mixers at the South Tacoma USO in South Park during the summer of 1942. The USO provided a variety of services for those in the military; chief among them were morale-boosting social activities. The South Tacoma USO building became the South Park Community Center after World War II. (Courtesy TPL.)

McKinley Playfield's day-camp offerings in the 1950s included this nod to the then-current popularity of all things Davy Crockett. The bulletin board advertised more fun in store for day campers, with a puppet show, story time, and a nature hike, as well as a program for junior park leaders.

Children of the Lincoln Park neighborhood pose with their decorated bikes on the street in front of Lincoln Park to advertise the following evening's Family Night, with activities and fun for all ages. The exact date of the photograph is unrecorded, but the youngster at the far left, whose placard proclaims, "I like Ike!", makes a date between 1953 and 1961 a possibility.

Summer fun on a hot day has changed very little in Wright Park over 50 years—water sports drew children then and now. In 1927, when South Yakima Avenue still bisected the park, the old wading pool and play equipment were situated uphill from their present location, and there was little difference in boys' and girls' knitted swimwear. By the 1970s, as an alternative to cooling off in the pool, a slippery slide offered neighborhood youngsters clad in T-shirts and shorts an afternoon's glee. Regardless of the decade, a boy in each photograph certainly appreciated the attention of the photographer.

Crowds thronged the 1937 Inter-Playfield Handcraft Exhibition held on August 26 in Wright Park, a city-wide festival that also featured a track meet and other activities. Handcrafts from the various playfield programs and community centers across the city of Tacoma were set up on wooden trestle tables in the park and then displayed, admired, and judged. Entries visible in the photograph above include wooden bookends, dollhouses, and paper artwork. The photograph below captures the intensity of the judging on the faces of, from left to right, Betty Worden, the grand-prize winner representing Lincoln Park, and two of the judges, Mr. and Mrs. Carl Evers.

Tacoma's parks were not the only locations in which to celebrate its programs and activities. In this undated photograph c. 1950, children from the various parks' recreation programs demonstrate their craft skills at long trestle tables set up along the curb on downtown's Broadway. The F. W. Woolworth store is visible at the end of the block on the other side of the street.

From left to right, Princess Lincoln Park, Mr. Lincoln Park, and Miss Lincoln Park pose for posterity in the Mighty Mite Hey Day contest at the South Park Day Camp in the summer of 1961. The youngsters, their identities otherwise unknown, must have enjoyed a warm, sunny day in Tacoma on the day of this photograph.

In 1962, a very popular community picnic tradition started at Point Defiance Park's Owen Beach that lasted over 20 years. That summer, the Metropolitan Park District and the Tacoma Chamber of Commerce jointly sponsored salmon bakes on a weekly basis as an event to link Tacoma with the larger regional events surrounding Seattle's 1962 World's Fair. The 1962 salmon bakes featured prices remarkable by today's standards and paper headdresses for all. Below, Eva Davis Stewart, who served from 1951 to 1975 as the first woman on the Board of Park Commissioners, poses with dinner. The salmon bakes of successive years were held at Owen Beach several times each summer and frequently featured fireworks, dancing, and other themed entertainment.

For decades, the Metropolitan Park District has offered recreational programs not just for children, but for a wide variety of interests spanning the generations. In cooperation with other community agencies, activities and educational experiences brought together people from all sectors of the city. In the 1960s photograph above, a Tacoma Suburban Lines charter bus awaits imminent departure, taking a group of sensibly shod active adults from South Park Community Center to Mount Rainier National Park. On the other end of the adult spectrum, representative teenagers from all of the city's high schools participated in the City Wide Youth Council in the 1960s and 1970s, a program cosponsored with the Tacoma School District.

Summer playfield supervisors of the 1930s dressed in white and wore armbands that identified them as playground directors. An unidentified man and woman, employed by the Metropolitan Park District's supervisor of recreation, pose with two young charges, also unidentified, during a break from play on a busy summer day. The whistle on a lanyard around the woman's neck would have been required equipment.

Playground leaders in the 1960s, identified only as Nancy (left) and Ebba (right), are more informally dressed in Metropolitan Park District jackets and badges as they assist two young charges with the check-out of basketballs. Many Tacoma teens recall past summer employment in the parks as an ideal first job.

Donna Thompson, a student at the University of Washington, worked for the Metropolitan Park District of Tacoma as a playground leader in the summer of 1947; she coached the Irving Playfield Teenage Fastball Club to the city championship with a winning combination of enthusiasm and strategy. In the photograph above, she works with a player to perfect his batting stance. Thompson served the park district as a playground leader for several summers. She also appears below, at the far right of the front row, in the group photograph of the playground leaders in the summer of 1948 in front of the South Park Community Center. Superintendent of public recreation Tom Lantz is the man in the suit in the middle of the front row. (Courtesy TPL and MPT.)

The Metropolitan Park District of Tacoma was instrumental in starting specialized recreation programs in the 1960s for children with mental and physical disabilities. Directed from South Park Community Center, the programs offered the opportunity for children across the city of Tacoma and beyond to participate in some of the ordinary rites of childhood, such as the pleasure of attending day camp. The photograph above records a parade led by camp leaders on the wooded grounds of South Park complete with newspaper hats and paper chains. Below, the royalty of 1967 Daffodil Queen Carol Parcheta, in full court regalia, and two of her Daffodil Princesses delights the day campers with an appearance by true Tacoma celebrities.

Richard Read of 3555 Roosevelt Avenue wore a clever costume in 1928 for one of the many playground theatricals popular throughout the city; a stage situated in the ravine in Lincoln Park was the venue for many of them. Young Read was captured for posterity by a photographer from Read Photo Service of the same address, so the junior thespian may have been posing for his father.

South Park in 1959 boasted play equipment to launch childhood imaginations. Although unidentified, these young riders could have imagined themselves on the trail with the Lone Ranger, their footwear notwithstanding. Their lunch awaits on the picnic tables to the left of the picture, while additional children play in a sandbox at the right.

Pet parades were a favorite pastime in the supervised playfield activities across the city of Tacoma. In cooperation with the Tacoma School District, the Metropolitan Park District established additional playfields and programs on many school-district properties, such as the old Central School grounds and Sherman Elementary and Mason Intermediate Schools, to name just two North End examples. These photographs from 1928 record a pet parade from Mason Intermediate School, above, that included not only dogs and cats, but goats, chickens, and rabbits—some led, some cajoled, some carried in baskets. The location pictured is the corner of North Twenty-sixth and Proctor Streets, looking east; Sanstrom's Department store is now a Radio Shack. The image below documents another such procession near Franklin School. Pet parades continued to be a prime feature of summer playfield activities well into the 1960s.

Five

PLAY BALL

Sports and athletics are now seen as an integral part of the programs and activities offered by the Metropolitan Park District of Tacoma, but that has not always been the case. In 1907, baseball players were told that neither McKinley nor Lincoln Park were available for the building of a ballpark. In 1909, the Metropolitan Park District asked the superintendent of public schools to have the teachers take up the matter of children running over grass in the parks. Citizens in some neighborhoods spoke out against baseball fields in their neighborhoods for fear that it would lower their property values.

These attitudes quickly changed as more and more people came to understand the importance of offering athletic opportunities to channel the energies of young people into worthwhile endeavors. Sports came to be viewed as a way to instill cooperation and teamwork in the young and were enthusiastically supported in the parks.

Tacoma's parks have been the setting for many kinds of competition: baseball, softball, pitching horseshoes, shooting marbles, bicycle races, croquet, archery, and tennis, just to name a few. Specialized facilities such as Heidelberg/Davis Sports Complex, Peck Field, South End Recreation Area, Titlow Pool, Stewart Heights Pool, and Meadow Park Golf Course were built to accommodate large team sports as well as individual instruction and enjoyment. Many of Tacoma's parks include basketball courts, tennis courts, and dedicated open space for citizens to enjoy their preferred sport during leisure time. A cooperative agreement between the park district and the Tacoma School District allows park district staff the opportunity to program school gymnasiums, fields, and pools for instructions and team sports when not utilized by school programs. This is the outgrowth of a 1944 program called the Tacoma Recreation Commission, when the schools and the parks formalized their relationship to provide the widest variety and greatest athletic opportunities for the citizens of Tacoma.

In 1923, the first National Marbles Tournament was held. Tacoma's representative was Lloyd Williamson, who no doubt inspired many future generations of Tacoma boys and girls to master the game where the object was to hit the opponent's "pip" out of a circle. These young men, seen practicing their shooting skills with intense concentration, may very well have been some of Tacoma's marble champions.

Organized marble tournaments were still held through the 1950s. This photograph from a Daffodil Tournament in Wright Park in 1959 shows many young contestants anxiously awaiting their opportunity to show their skills while the judges prepare the playing fields, specially set up for this event.

In 1927, these two young men work hard to develop their horseshoe pitching skills, most likely inspired by Tacoma horseshoe champion Floyd Sayre. Sayre was the state horseshoe champion in 1924 and the president of the Tacoma Horseshoe Pitchers Association in 1925. A Commercial Horseshoe League sponsored by local businesses was begun by the park district in the 1920s to encourage business sponsorship of the game.

Even though the game of horseshoes lost some of its popularity by the 1940s, it is obvious that this group of young men in the 1950s is intent on perfecting their skills. At one time, there were more than 15 courts located in playgrounds throughout the city. Tacoma is also credited with inventing the game of barnyard golf, an 18-peg course set up to be played like a round of golf.

The sport of pitching horseshoes evolved from the ancient game of quoits, one of the five games in the ancient Greek pentathlon. Over time, the iron rings or quoits were replaced with horseshoes. By 1925, the National Horseshoe Pitchers Association formed, and Tacoma players were a part of this national trend. Horseshoes were wildly popular in the 1920s and 1930s. Courts quickly sprang up in parks throughout Tacoma. Horseshoe courts were built in Central School grounds in 1925 and were quickly followed by courts in Point Defiance Park. This photograph commemorates the

Northwest Horseshoe Picnic in Point Defiance Park on July 12, 1931. For that event, the Tacoma Horseshoe Pitching Association invited Putt Mossman, world-champion fancy horseshoe-pitching crown holder, to compete against local teams. Putt and his sister Bessie can be seen in the right-hand side of this picture dressed in white slacks and tops. Not only were Putt and Bessie world famous "ringers," but they were also trick motorcycle riders. (Courtesy Vennard and Jan Lahti.)

The open lawns in many of Tacoma's parks made the perfect location to play croquet, a sport requiring flat open space, simple wood mallets, wooden balls, and wire hoops. The young men in the picture above from 1928 are obviously paying close attention to the hit being made by the boy on the far left.

The first annual bicycle meet, sponsored by the *Tacoma Times* and the park district, was held in 1938. These competitions generally involved an obstacle course as well as speed contests and were held in various parks around the city. The young lady preparing to fire the starting pistol stands in the bowl area of Point Defiance Park. Every child who participated received a Double Cola and a Hambone candy bar.

In 1940, the park district sponsored a three-day bike ride to Twanoh State Park on the Hood Canal. The first leg of the trip involved the group riding their bicycles across the newly completed Narrows Bridge. Virginia Greening Niskar of Tacoma remembers participating in this ride and tying a pillow to her bicycle seat "when deemed necessary."

A second bike trip to Twanoh State Park was held in 1941, but this time the riders took a ferry across the Narrows. "Galloping Gertie" had fallen into Puget Sound since their last ride. Here a recreation leader can be seen packing the playground department truck with needed food and camping supplies for the long bicycle trip and overnight stay at the state park.

Just five years after Point Defiance Park became an official Tacoma park in 1905, tennis courts were installed on the grounds to accommodate members of the public who wanted to enjoy this lively sport. Courts were soon installed in several other city parks, and the park district sponsored numerous city-wide competitions. Here, from left to right, the 1927 park board champions, Grafe Hibberly, Alberta Edtl, unidentified, George O'Leary, and unidentified, pose for the camera.

In 1940, the recreation department organized a Junior Olympics program to encourage participation in a wide variety of sports. Children from all around the city participated in games including softball, ping pong, soccer, swimming, hand lacrosse, and track-and-field competitions. Here the paddle tennis champions pose by the lake in Wright Park.

Tacoma's first golf course, Tacoma Golf Club, was established in 1894. A second course was built in South Tacoma, but it was forced to close in 1904 due to rising land values in that section of town. Fortunately for golfers in the south end of town, Meadow Park Golf Course was built in 1915 to accommodate the growing interest in golf. Meadow Park's 165-acre course was privately owned but open to the public. Tacoma's interest in golf continued to grow, as can been seen in this 1928 photograph of young men intently focused on the golfer's performance. After many years of private ownership, the park district purchased Meadow Park in 1962.

PUBLIC LINKS

The Meadow Park Golf Course

Announcement of Opening

The second nine of this course will be opened Sunday, Nov. 14, and the 18-hole course will be opened 2 weeks later.

Annual tickets will be dated Jan. 1, 1916, on sale at Kimball Gun Store or the links, $12, COVERING GREENS FEES, CLUBHOUSE AND LOCKER.

Single Game—18 Holes—Only 25c

American Lake car—to city limits—5c fare.

The sport of baseball has a long tradition in Tacoma. The Tacoma Invincibles of 1874 may have only existed as a team for 12 days, but their legacy inspired many a young person, such as these boys seen playing in Wright Park. Baseball and softball fields are an important component of many of Tacoma's parks, with the park district's recreation department organizing league play throughout the city.

To encourage interest in the game and to improve the skills of youth in the community, the recreation department has offered many opportunities over the years for young people to learn from the professionals. Here Earl Kuper demonstrates a hook slide for young baseball-star hopefuls. Kuper played catcher for the Tacoma Tigers from 1946 to 1948.

Tacoma's first baseball stadium, Tacoma Athletic Field, located at South Fourteenth Street and Sprague Avenue, was completed in 1907 and had a 7,500-person capacity. Updated in 1913, this stadium offered a location for players like the men in this 1927 picture to show off their skills. In 1950, Roger Peck, owner of the field, worked with the Tacoma–Pierce County Softball Association to develop the softball facility now called Peck Field.

Prior to developing the old Tacoma Athletic Field into Peck Field, it was used as a midget-auto racetrack. The grand opening of the track was held on May 10, 1946. The cars raced under floodlights, and the races started at 8:15 p.m. General admission was $1.50; children and servicemen were admitted for 75¢. The old baseball diamond can be seen inside the course's oval track. (Courtesy TPL.)

In 1955–1956, the park district built Heidelberg Park on South Nineteenth Street. Even though naming the field for a local brewing company was very controversial at the time, Heidelberg has proven to be an excellent location for baseball and softball players from around the community to test their skills. The Heidelberg Brewing Company donated the majority of the money needed to build the sport complex. This aerial photograph from the 1960s presents a wonderful bird's-eye view of the area. Heidelberg is seen in the foreground to the left, and Cheney Stadium (built in 1960) is in the center. Foss High School (1973) was not built yet. Tacoma's soapbox derby track can be seen to the right of both fields. This racecourse for homemade, engineless cars was built by the Kiwanis organization in 1957. On the far right of the photograph is Bantz Boulevard, now the route of Highway 16.

This aerial photograph of Peck Field clearly shows the four softball fields radiating out from the center of the park. One of the selling points for this new sports complex was lights so that games could go on well into the evening. In 1950, the admission was 25¢ for adults and 9¢ for children. The price is still reasonable, with adult admission of $1 in 2007.

Heidelberg Park's two softball fields can be seen in the foreground, with two tee-ball fields just behind them. In the distance is the baseball field. In 2002, the baseball field was dedicated to Bob Maguinez, longtime player, coach, umpire, and athletic supervisor at Heidelberg. The name of the park was changed to Heidelberg/Davis to honor Norman Davis, president of Heidelberg Brewing Company when the brewery donated the money to build the park.

The chilly waters of Puget Sound did not deter these 12 hardy competitors from a two-mile swim from Vashon Island to the pavilion at Point Defiance Park on September 26, 1926. The race, sponsored by the park district, was won by Gerhard Bahr in the time of one hour and two minutes. The only female contestant, 15-year-old Alexina Slater, took fourth place.

The beach and picnic area in Point Defiance Park now called Owen Beach was named in 1959 to honor Floyd Owen, a 47-year park district employee. This beach was used by early campers and picnickers long before it was formally named. In the 1930s, amenities including a bathhouse and concession building were added. Lifeguard Dale Latham stands guard over swimmers in Puget Sound in 1954.

Prior to the construction of public swimming pools, residents cooled off on hot summer days in natural bodies of water, such as the lagoon at Titlow Beach, Wapato Lake, or Puget Sound. In 1955, Titlow Pool, a 165-foot-by-75-foot heated swimming pool, was completed at Titlow Park. This heated pool was reported to be one of the country's finest and, as this photograph attests, one of Tacoma's most popular.

Competitive swimmers have enjoyed Titlow Pool for training and competition since its opening on June 4, 1955. Here Tacoma Swim Club coach Dick Hannula works with potential Olympic champions in 1977. Hannula founded the Tacoma Swim Club in 1955 and served as head coach until 1998. He was inducted into the Swimming Hall of Fame in 1987.

A second outdoor pool was built in 1958. The South End Swimming Pool at East Fifty-sixth and D Streets was unique in shape. Its T-shaped layout was designed to accommodate more people for recreational swims as well as provide more teaching stations for the popular Learn-to-Swim Program. A separate wading pool provided shallow water for children under the age of five. As a certified 50-meter pool, swim meets could be accommodated at this facility. Even though many repairs were tried over the years, the South End Pool continued to leak larger and larger volumes of water. It was removed and replaced in 2002 with the very popular Stewart Heights Leisure Pool, complete with waterslide, lazy river, and water toys for children of all ages to enjoy.

In a community surrounded by water, the citizens of Tacoma have come to rely on the park district as an important provider of swim lessons. Aquatics staff members teach swimming lessons for children and adults at the two park district-owned outdoor pools during the summer months and in the indoor pools at People's Community Center, the Centre at Norpoint, and Eastside Pool, as well as Tacoma School District–owned facilities during the remainder of the year. At right, instructor Vic Holmes shows Candi Meyers the basic strokes before she enters the water. Below, Karen Ramstad teaches Debbi Johnson how to float at South End Pool.

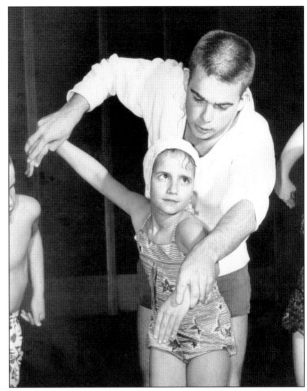

Whether one prefers to spend time in Tacoma's parks quietly relaxing and enjoying the scenery, as in the picture below of the pond in Wright Park, or engaging in one's favorite sport or activity, as is the jauntily clad young man in the picture at left, be assured that Tacoma has a park to fit one's needs. The citizens of Tacoma have recognized the importance of parks to the community's well-being for over 100 years. It is a significant heritage of beauty, natural history, and stewardship inherited from past generations and bequeathed to those of the future.

INDEX OF PHOTOGRAPHS

The authors are grateful to all who allowed use of their photographs to bring the history of Tacoma's parks to life. All photographs not credited are part of the collection of the Metropolitan Park District of Tacoma.

The photographs of the Tacoma Public Library's Northwest Room are identified below:

ACROSS AMERICA, PEOPLE ARE DISCOVERING SOMETHING WONDERFUL. *THEIR HERITAGE.*

Arcadia Publishing is the leading local history publisher in the United States. With more than 3,000 titles in print and hundreds of new titles released every year, Arcadia has extensive specialized experience chronicling the history of communities and celebrating America's hidden stories, bringing to life the people, places, and events from the past. To discover the history of other communities across the nation, please visit:

www.arcadiapublishing.com

Customized search tools allow you to find regional history books about the town where you grew up, the cities where your friends and family live, the town where your parents met, or even that retirement spot you've been dreaming about.